Early Potty
ABCs

About This Book:

Early Potty ABCs

Copyright © 2025 by Jillian Quay

Book design by Jodi McPhee

ISBN: 979-8-9986004-0-1 (Hard cover)
ISBN: 979-8-9986004-1-8 (Paperback)

www.EarlyPottyABCs.com

Printed in the United States

Early Potty ABCs

by Jillian Quay

illustrated by Rudra Bose

TRUCKEE ROSE PRESS ♥ TRUCKEE, CALIFORNIA

Dear Reader,

"Early pottying" (or Elimination Communication / "EC") is a beneficial and intuitive practice for you and your baby, even if it's something you do part-time. For example, you can offer the potty once a day when your baby first wakes up. Saving one diaper a day means saving the cost of 365 diapers a year and 365 diapers from going into a landfill.

Before disposable diapers were invented and marketed to parents, parents used early potty techniques and had their children potty-trained at 18 months.

The best time to start early pottying is between birth and 4 months; however, this method can be introduced anytime up to 18 months. **Using this method, you can avoid some or almost all smelly diaper changes, and your walking toddler will have the potential to walk himself or herself to the potty when needed.**

Please keep in mind that there is no right or wrong way to early potty. You can listen to your baby's natural signals and follow your little one's lead. View the early potty method as a journey of learning and bonding with your child. Check out **www.EarlyPottyABCs.com** for more resources.

Warm wishes to you and your baby on your early potty journey!

–Jillian

Tip for Success

Communication is at the heart of early pottying.
Use the same cue sound each time — you'll be
surprised how quickly your baby catches on.

Here are some sounds to try:

- The letter "P" sound (easy for a baby to duplicate)
- "Psss" or "Psh" (the sound of running water)

These can work well for a #2 elimination:

- Gentle clearing of the throat (easy for a young baby to duplicate)
- "Grrr" or "Pooo"…or choose another one that works for you!

Aa

is for animal play
at potty time.

Puppets and favorite stuffed animals can help you and your child relax. Use them to role-play and tell stories, or hold them for comfort.

Bb

is for **books**
at potty time.

Potty time can also be a special time for reading together.
Keep a stack of favorite books next to your potty station.

Cc

is for clap
when there's a catch!

A "catch" is a time to celebrate. Smile and clap, even
if it only happens sometimes.

(*A catch is a successful pee or poop.*)

Dd

is for diaper savings.

Save money by using
fewer diapers.

Ee

is for the Earth.

Early pottying is better for our environment.
Diapers are made of plastic and can take
500 years to decompose!

Ff

is for family involvement.

Do you and your child enjoy early pottying?
Make sure to involve other caregivers and share the ABCs
of early pottying with grandparents, siblings, daycare,
and preschool teachers so that they can support you.

Gg

is for go outside
and offer potty time.

The fresh air outside can help a young one relax. Find a private place near a tree or a rock. Cue and sign "potty" once you find your favorite spot.

Hh

is for top **hat** potty for newborns (0-4 months old).

You can try the potty as early as the day your baby is born! A plastic top hat or a similar shape makes an easy early baby potty.

Ii

is for potty independence much sooner.

Learning to use the potty
early is easier for kids than
learning it later.

Jj

is for joy when
there is a "catch!"

Big baby smiles after a "catch" are the best.

Kk

is for little kid potty from 4 months old and up.

Young babies will need front and back support while on this kind of mini potty. Older babies can sit up by themselves.

Ll

is for **look** for common signals.

When they need to use the potty, babies may:

- ♥ try to escape the carrier
- ♥ grab their diaper or pants
- ♥ be still
- ♥ or be fussy

Mm

is for misses.

Misses will happen, and they are okay! They are a part of the learning journey. Make a cue sound, even when there is a "miss." Say, "Next time, we will use the potty."

Nn

is for nap time.

Potty time before napping can lead to a more restful sleep. Potty time after nap time is an ideal time for a "catch."

Oo

is for **offer** the potty.

Offer the potty at diaper
changes, undressing, and
after any milk or food.

(Basically, offer it during any transition!)

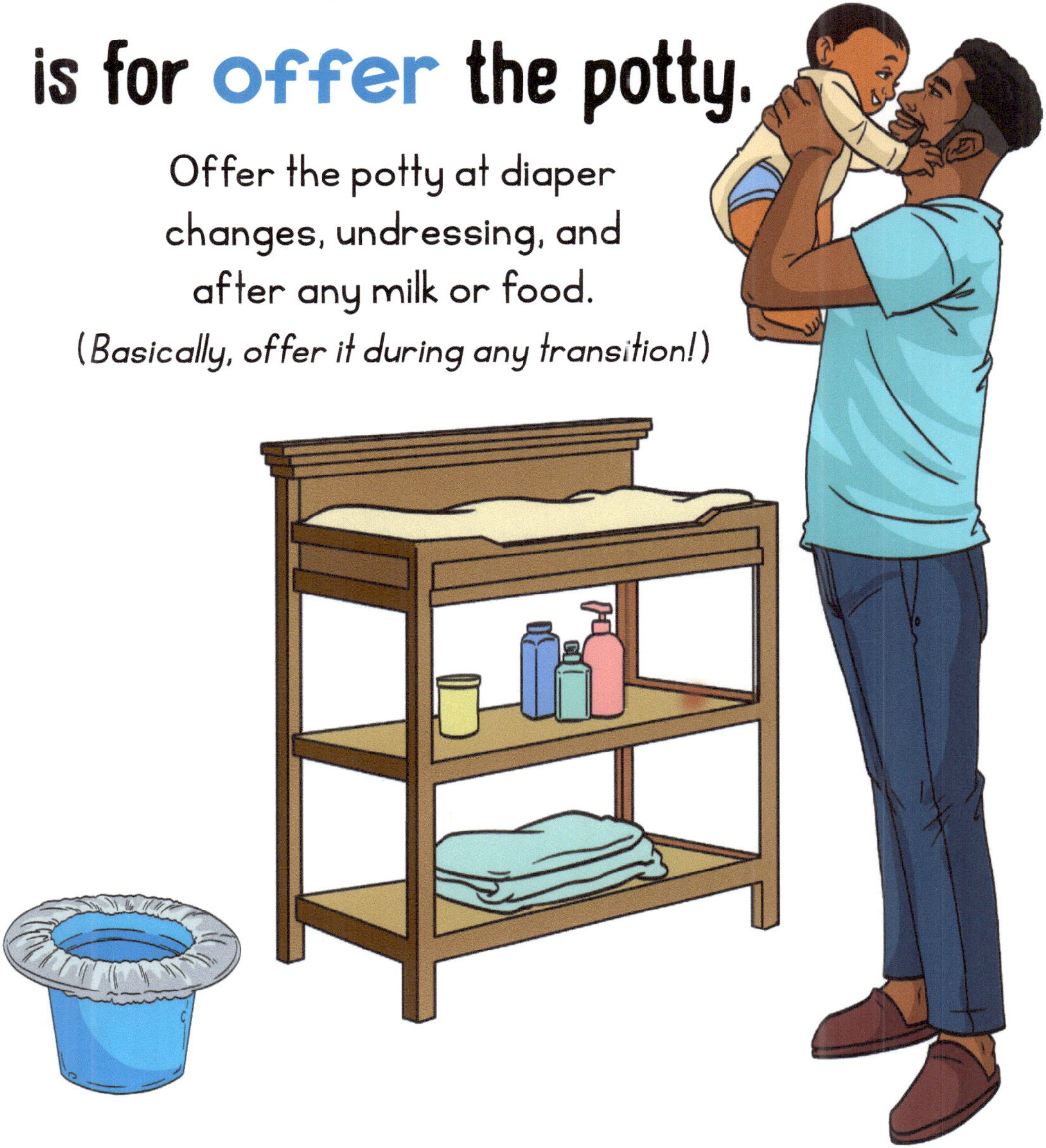

Pp

is for positions
that support baby.

Here are some favorite
early potty positions:

Qq

is for act quickly
at any potty sign.

Sometimes, you will
need to move
quickly to
be successful.

Rr

is for respect.
Respect a "no."

Listen to your child and try again later.

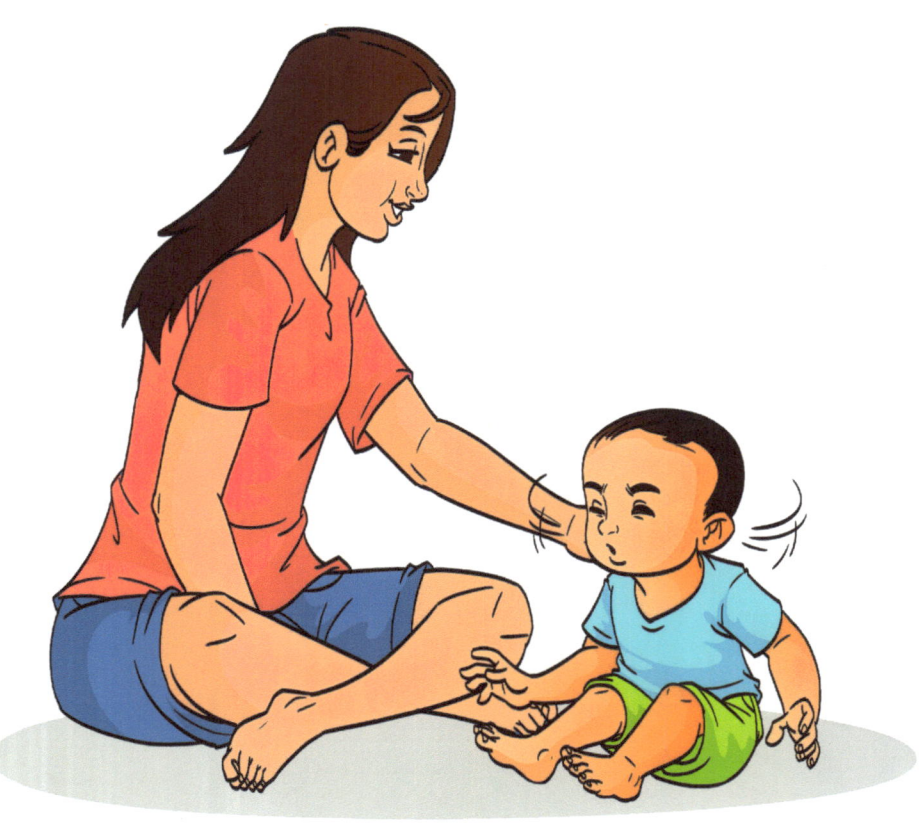

Ss

is for sign.

Sign "potty" every time baby tries to potty. Make this shape with your hand and gently shake it from side to side. Say the word "potty" or "toilet" at the same time as you sign.

(When your baby first tries to sign, it might
look like a little wave of the fist.)

Tt

is for **toilets**.

Try many types: little potties, portable seats,
seat reducers, and public toilets.

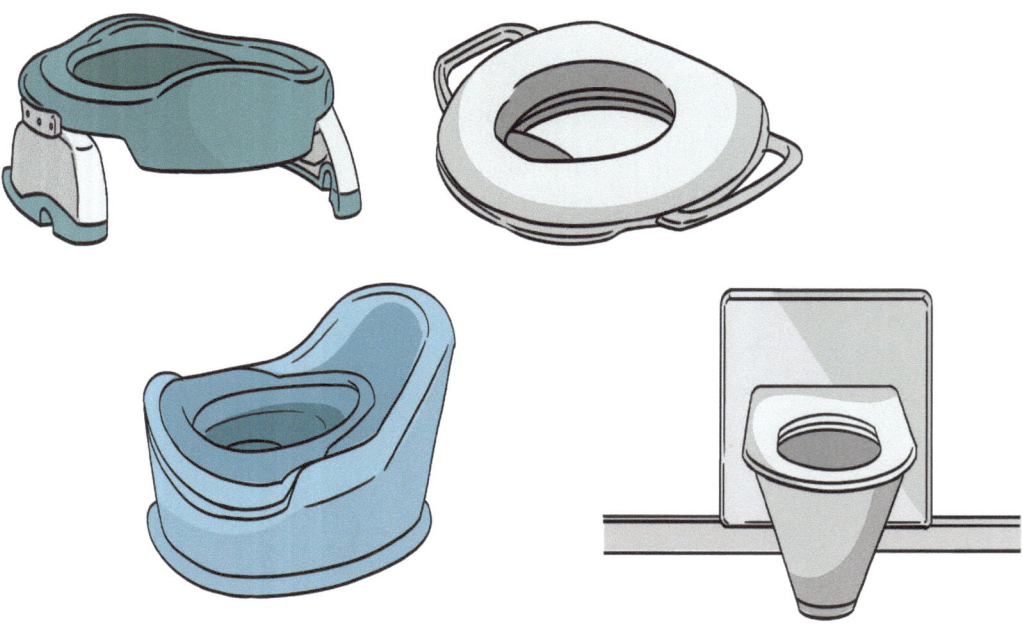

Uu
is for undies.

Dress your baby with underwear sooner
for faster potty learning.

Vv

is for vacation.

Take a small potty when traveling
by car, train, or airplane.

Ww

is for **wake** up potty time.

First thing in the morning and after a nap are easy times for a catch.

is for X marks the spot
for an outside pee.

Also, stay fle**X**ible and rela**X**ed—
if one thing isn't working, try another.

Yy

is for you
can do this!

Early potty learning is a journey.
The process is different for everyone!

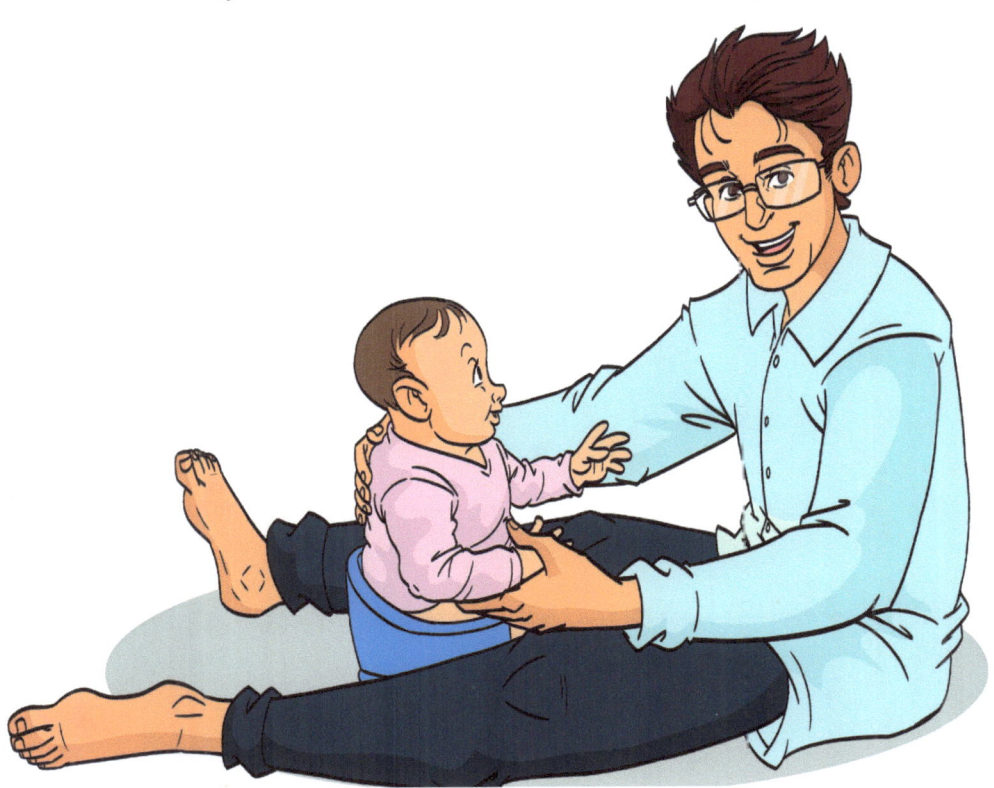

Zz

is for Zzzzz.

Shhhh, baby is sleeping.